CAT

CUTIES

(and kittens to coo over)

Karen Prince

HYLAS

Hylas Publishing
Publisher: Sean Moore
Creative Director: Karen Prince
Designer: Pakpoom Rojanapisit
Editor: Myrsini Stephanides
Proofreader: Ginger Skinner

First published by
Hylas Publishing
129 Main Street, Irvington,
New York 10533
www.hylaspublishing.com

Compilation Copyright © Hylas Publishing 2004
Library of Congress Data available upon request

ISBN 1-59258-109-9

Set in News701 BT and Snell Special Script
Printed and bound in Hong Kong

Distributed in the U.S.A. by the National Book Network
and in Canada by Kate Walker & Company

2   4   6   8   10   9   7   5   3   1

C A T

C U T I E S

www.hylaspublishing.com

HYLAS

"The more people
I meet, the more
I like my cat."

Anonymous

"Way down deep,

we're all motivated

by the same urges.

Cats have the courage

to live by them."

Jim Davis

"Cat: A pygmy
lion who loves
mice, hates dogs,
and patronizes
human beings."

Oliver Herford

"The cat
is domestic only
as far as suits
its own ends."

H.H. Munro

"I've met many
thinkers and many cats,
but the wisdom of cats
is infinitely superior."

Hippolyte Taine

"Prowling his own quiet
backyard or asleep by the fire,
he is still only a whisker
away from the wilds."

Jean Burden

"An ordinary
kitten will ask
more questions
than any five-
year-old."

Carl Van

"As every
cat owner
knows, nobody
owns a cat."

Ellen Perry

"If cats

could talk,

they wouldn't."

Nan Porter

"By associating
with the cat,
one only risks
becoming richer."

Colette

"Intelligence
in the cat
is underrated."

Louis Wain

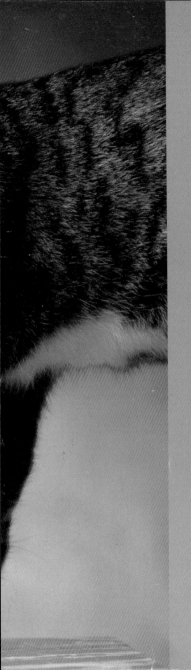

"As we all know,
cats now rule
the world."

John R.F. Breen

"Of all God's creatures,

there is only one that cannot

be made the slave of the lash. That

one is the cat. If man could be crossed

with a cat, it would improve man,

but it would deteriorate the cat."

Mark Twain

"Cat people are different,

to the extent that they

generally are not conformists.

How could they be, with

a cat running their lives?"

Louis J.

"There is nothing
sweeter than his
peace when
at rest, for there
is nothing brisker
than his life
when in motion."

Christopher Smart

"If you are worthy
of its affection,
a cat will be your
friend, but never
your slave."

Theophile Gautier

"Kitten: A small homicidal
muffin on legs; affects human
sensibilities to the point
of endowing the most
wanton and ruthless acts
of destruction with near-mythical
overtones of cuteness.
Not recommended for beginners.
Get at least two."

Anonymous

"Kittens are born with their
eyes shut. They open them in about
six days, take a look around, then
close them again for the better
part of their lives."

Stephen Baker

"I believe cats
to be spirits come
to earth. A cat, I am sure,
could walk on a cloud
without coming through."

Jules Verne

"In ancient times, cats
were worshiped
as gods; they
have never
forgotten this."

Unknown

"Cats are the ultimate narcissists.
You can tell this because
of all the time they spend on personal
grooming. Dogs aren't like this.
A dog's idea of personal grooming
is to roll in a dead fish."

James Gorman

"I love cats because
I enjoy my home; and little
by little, they become
its visible soul."

Jean Cocteau

"Dogs come when
they're called; cats
take a message
and get back
to you later."

Mary Bly

"Beware
of people who
dislike cats."

Proverb

"Women and cats will
do as they please, and men
and dogs should relax
and get used to the idea."

Anonymous

"A cat's hearing apparatus
is built to allow the human
voice to easily go in one
ear and out the other."

Stephen Baker

"Dogs are eternally
grateful that
humans exist;
cats, however,
are simply mildly
appreciative!"

Carl Brizzi

"Cats are intended
to teach us that
not everything
in nature has
a purpose."

Garrison Keillor

"There are many
intelligent species
in the universe. They
are all owned by cats."

Anonymous

"Cats are absolute
individuals, with their
own ideas about everything,
including the people they own."

John Dingman

"We cannot,
without becoming
cats, perfectly
understand
the cat mind."

St. George Mivart

"It's very hard
to be polite
if you're a cat."

Anonymous

"Dogs believe
they are human.
Cats believe
they are God."

Anonymous

"There's no need
for a piece of sculpture
in a home that has a cat."

Wesley Bates

"Cats are
connoisseurs
of comfort."

James Herriot

"Dogs have
owners; cats
have staff."

Anonymous

"Most cats, when
they are out, want
to be in, and vice versa,
and often simultaneously."

Louis F. Camuti

"My cat does not
talk as respectfully
to me as I do to her."

Colette

"The ideal
of calm exists
in a sitting cat."

Jules Reynard

"Every life

should have

nine cats."

Anonymous

"No amount of time can erase
the memory of a good cat,
and no amount of masking tape
can ever totally remove
his fur from your couch."

Leo Dworken

"Some people say that cats
are sneaky, evil, and cruel. True,
and they have many other
fine qualities as well."

Missy Dizick

"Time spent
with cats
is never
wasted."

Colette

"The smart
cat doesn't let
on that he is."

H.G. Frommer

"It always gives

me a shiver

when I see a cat

seeing what

I can't see."

Eleanor Farjeon

"A cat has absolute emotional
honesty: human beings,
for one reason or another,
may hide their feelings,
but a cat does not."

Ernest Hemingway

"Her function
is to sit and
be admired."

Georgina S. Gates

"I love cats because
I enjoy my home;
and little by little,
they become
its visible soul."

Jean Cocteau

"The cat seldom interferes
with other people's rights.
His intelligence keeps
him from doing many
of the fool things that
complicate life."

Carl V. Vechten

"Everything I know I learned from my cat: When you're hungry, eat. When you're tired, nap in a sunbeam. When you go to the vet's, pee on your owner."

Gary Smith

"One must love
a cat on its
own terms."

Paul Gray

"Cats are kindly
masters, just
so long as you
remember
your place."

Paul Gray

"After scolding one's
cat, one looks into its face
and is seized by the ugly
suspicion that it understood
every word. And has filed
it for reference."

Charlotte Gray

"When I play with my cat,

how do I know that

she is not passing

time with me rather

than I with her?"

Montaigne

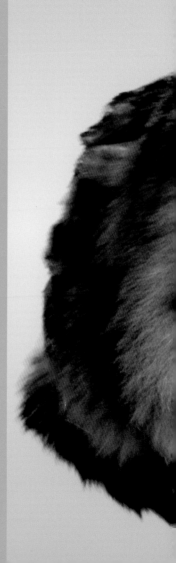

"The trouble
with cats is that
they've got
no tact."

P.G. Wodehouse

"The cat has
too much
spirit to have
no heart."

Ernest Menaul

"Cats are a tonic, they
are a laugh, they are a cuddle,
they are at least pretty just
about all of the time
and beautiful some
of the time."

Roger Caras

"Of all animals, the cat alone
attains to the contemplative
life. He regards the wheel
of existence from without,
like the Buddha."

Andrew Lang

PICTURE CREDITS